Core of Wisdom

by

Adnan I. Qureshi, M.D.

Bloomington, IN  Milton Keynes, UK

authorHOUSE®

AuthorHouse™
1663 Liberty Drive, Suite 200
Bloomington, IN 47403
www.authorhouse.com
Phone: 1-800-839-8640

AuthorHouse™ UK Ltd.
500 Avebury Boulevard
Central Milton Keynes, MK9 2BE
www.authorhouse.co.uk
Phone: 08001974150

First published by AuthorHouse 12/20/2006

ISBN: 978-1-4259-7033-8 (sc)

Library of Congress Control Number: 2006909534

Printed in the United States of America
Bloomington, Indiana

This book is printed on acid-free paper.

Core of Wisdom

by

Adnan I. Qureshi MD

Preface

Quotations are like tools, gauges, meters, warning lights, instruments and controls, which are essential for the smooth operation of our life's vehicle. Because of their depth and poignancy, they serve as palatable cooked-and-packaged food, and they save us the hassle of collecting ingredients and cooking them ourselves. The minimum they do for us is to widen our list of options to handle different situations of life and be better prepared for all eventualities.

Adnan I. Qureshi MD

Dedication

I dedicate this book to my beloved wife, Aasma Qureshi, who is a great source of inspiration for me. I thank Mr. Shaukat Bhatti for his very valuable assistance in compiling this book. I also thank Drs. Mustapha A. Ezzeddine and Afshin A. Divani for providing photographs for this book. I also want to thank PDPhoto.org for providing some of the public domain photographs used in the book.

This book contains thoughts on the following subjects

ACCEPTANCE
ACHIEVEMENT
ACHIEVING BEYOND DESTINY
ACTIONS
ADVERSITY
ADVICE
ALLIES
ALWAYS
AMBIGUITY
AMBITION
ANONYMITY
ARTIST
ASSUMPTION
AVAILABILITY
BASIC RIGHTS
BIG FISH
BRIDGES
CARING VERSUS OVERBEARING
CHANGE
CHANGE OF SYSTEM
CLINICAL TRIAL
COMPETITION
CONCESSIONS
CONFESSION
CONFIDENCE VERSUS ARROGANCE
CONFLICT
CONFLICT RESOLUTION
CONTEMPT
CONTENTMENT AND DISCONTENTMENT
CONTRIBUTION
CORRUPTION
CRACKS
CRISIS MANAGEMENT
CRITIQUE
CURIOSITY

DEAL
DESIRE
DESTINY
DESPERATION
DIPLOMACY
DISTORTION
DIVERSITY
DREAMS
EATING
EFFORT
EMOTIONS
EXCESS
EXCELLENCE
EXCUSES
EXPANSION OF ORGANIZATION
EXPERIENCE
EXTERNAL THREATS
EXTREMISM
EVOLUTION
FACE
FALL
FAME
FATIGUE
FIGHT
FIRST RESPONSE
FITTING IN
FLAG
FLEXIBILITY
FREEDOM
FRIEND
FUNERAL
FUTURE
GENEROSITY
GLITTER
GREED
GREATNESS
GOALS

GUARANTEE
GUILT
GYMNASIUM
HAND
HATRED
HONOR
HOPE
HUMAN PSYCHE
HUMAN RIGHTS
IGNORANCE
IMPORTANCE OF NEGATIVE PHENOMENA
IN AND OUT
INCOMPETENCE
INDECISIVENESS
INERTIA
INEVITABLY BAD
INNER PEACE
INSECURITY
INTERPRETATION
INSTINCT
INTEGRATION
JUDGE
KEY
KNOWLEDGE
LEADERSHIP
LOSS
LOVE
LOYALTY AND INTEGRITY
MARRIAGE
MODERN MEDICINE
MORTALITY
NEGOTIATION
NEW IDEAS
OPPORTUNITIES
ORGANIZATION
OUTCOME
PERSEVERANCE

POLITICS
POWER
PRACTICAL
PRESS
PREVENTION
PRIDE
PRODUCTIVITY
PROFESSIONAL COMPETITION
PROPER PERSPECTIVE
RANDOMIZATION
REASSURANCE
RELATIONSHIP
RESPECT VERSUS POPULARITY
RESPONSE
REVOLUTION
ROCK BOTTOM
RHYTHM
SACRIFICE
SEARCH FOR GOD
SEARCH FOR HEROES
SELF-INTEREST
SELF-RELIANCE
SELFISHNESS VERSUS KINDNESS
SERMONS
SHADOW OF DOUBT
SHIFTING OF ANGER
SHRINE
SINCERITY
SINS
SMALL STEPS
SMILE
SORROW
STABILITY
STABLE MARRIAGE
STATISTICS
STATUS QUO
STRESS

SUCCESS AND FAILURE
SPECTATOR SPORT
SUNRISE AND SUNSET
TACTICIAN
TAKEN FOR GRANTED
TALENT
TEACHERS
TEAM
TEMPTATION
TIME
TRUST
TRUTH
UNCERTAINTY
UNIVERSE
UNTHINKABLE
VALUABLE
VISION AND DEDICATION
VISIONARY
VICTORY
VULNERABILITY
WAR AND PEACE
WISDOM
WORLD ORDER
WORD AND ACTION

<u>ACCEPTANCE</u>
- Acceptance is not always voluntary; sometimes, it is the only way to avoid enforcement.

<u>ACHIEVEMENT</u>

- Achievement is delineated by the boundaries of time, ambition, and cost.

ACHIEVING BEYOND DESTINY

Rules for achieving beyond destiny
- Do not preach ethics; live it.
- Do not turn away from a challenge; face it.
- Do not shy away from responsibility; own it.
- Do not demand respect; earn it.
- Do not let temptation lead you astray; fight it.
- Do not scoff at valuable critique; consider it.
- There is no substitute for hard work and persistence; reward it.
- True leadership is beyond titles; command it.
- Quantum leaps require seeing what is not visible; imagine it.
- Greater destination is always set uphill; visualize it.
- Sacrifice is necessary for any great achievement; respect it.
- Sincere advice is a rare commodity; seek it.
- A legacy that you inherit must be dynamic; continue it.
- Trust is an important ingredient for all relationships; build it.
- People look up to leaders for guidance and even comfort; provide it.

- Someone besides you can have a good idea; accept it.
- God helps those who help themselves; believe it.

ACTIONS
- Actions driven by necessity must not lose grace in conduct.

ADVERSITY
- Adversity teaches us not only about others around us, but ourselves, as well.

- Adversity appears more daunting than it actually is, and prosperity appears more distant than it actually is.

- Beneath every stone of adversity lies a part of the map to prosperity. Turn enough of those around, and you will be able to piece together the road map to prosperity.
- Adversity is the mother of humanity. The worst adversity conceives the best humanity.

ADVICE

- Seek counsel regularly, but learn to judge it on merit. The best counsel provides an objective perspective of the situation and empowers you to choose the proper direction. The worst advice provides an emotional perspective of the situation, decides the direction for you, and impairs your power to make any decision.

ALLIES

- Powerful allies seek the same. No one will shake your hand if you cannot stand upright by yourself.
- External alliances are preceded by internal strength.
- A master tactician is the one who gets time to be on his side.

ALWAYS

- You always have a choice, regardless of how hard or limited it may be. You always have something good to rejoice over, regardless of the magnitude of surrounding adversity. You always receive praise for your work, regardless of credit lost to others.

AMBIGUITY

- Ambiguous decision today, confused action tomorrow.

AMBITION

- Morality is the reins, and faith is the saddle on the horse of ambition. To lack either is to lack both control and comfort throughout the journey.

- It is better to have no ambition rather than ambition without morality. The latter is like an untamed horse without reins, which is more likely to hurt others, and eventually, yourself.
- Blind ambition is blind both to loyalty and sincerity.
- Blind ambition is the horse that pulls our chariot up and subsequently down the mountain of success. The stronger the horse, the faster the journey is on both sides of the mountain.
- Ambition without acceptance is perfectionism; and perfectionism is the enemy of satisfaction.

ANONYMITY
- Anonymity is the face of great deeds and great sins.

ARTIST
- A true artist can make you enter his world without effort and imprison you there for an eternity.
- A great artist is the one who knows you even without meeting you.

ASSUMPTION
- Assumption is the mother of confusion.
- Assume nothing and plan for everything. It takes just one pin hiding under the blanket of assumption to burst the whole bubble inflated from endless computations.

AVAILABILITY
- Availability is the door to opportunity. Open it frequently, but selectively.

BASIC RIGHTS

- All political systems, including capitalism, feudalism, socialism, and monarchy, can work, provided they promulgate, preserve, and protect basic human rights.

BIG FISH

- A big fish in a small pond and a small fish in a big pond seek the same; to be a big fish in a big pond.

BRIDGES

- Each of us is an island connected to those around us by invisible bridges. Build, not burn, bridges, as they are essential for our existence, and you will cease to exist if you choose to burn all of them at the same time.

CARING VERSUS OVERBEARING

- Overbearing parents and spouses allow happiness only at their terms, while caring parents and spouses allow happiness at any reasonable terms.

CHANGE

- We overestimate our ability to change and underestimate our ability to adapt.
- Change occurs in three directions: expansion, regression, and redistribution. Change in any direction is acceptable, as long as it connects with a common origin.

- An extremely strong bond exists between life and change. Each life begins by bringing a message of change, and it ends by leaving a message of change. To stop change is to stop life.
- The only constant in the equation of life is the unquantifiable delta of change.
- Change is an enemy of comfort and a friend of success.
- Restless souls are driven by a constant desire for change; not necessarily a desire for peace.

- Change is triggered by baseline adversity, fueled by potential prosperity, and supported by surrounding intensity. People are ready for change when they are ready to walk through an uncharted path to unknown destination.

CHANGE OF SYSTEM
- Do not destroy a system without providing an alternate. This is a mistake commonly made during coup d'etats, takeovers, and invasions. Place emphasis on effective replacement rather than radical displacement.

CLINICAL TRIAL

- A clinical trial is an endeavor where every attempt is made to optimize the quality and quantity of expected learning, prior to venturing into the unknown.

COMPETITION

- We keep competing for control of existing resources, while alternate resources remain unexplored. The spirit of competition can be the enemy of diversification.

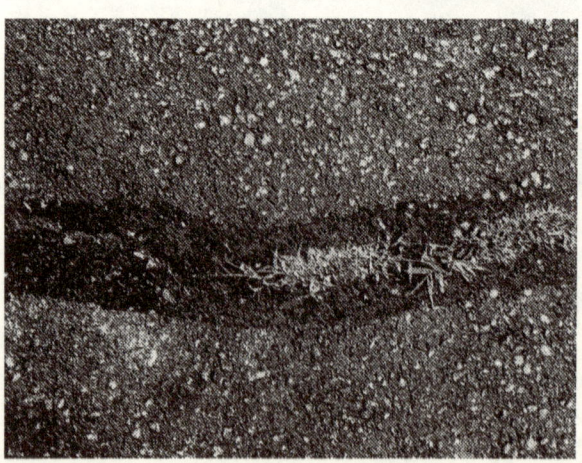

CONCESSIONS
- Political concessions are like spared weeds; comfortable today, unpredictable tomorrow.

CONFESSION
- Mistakes cannot be remedied by excuses. The only way forward is by admission and solution.

CONFIDENCE VERSUS ARROGANCE
- Be confident, but not arrogant! Confidence seeks to inspire, and arrogance seeks to humiliate others.
- The spotlight on the stage of life can blind you to friend and foe. Make sure that you periodically step off the stage to remain linked to reality.

CONFLICT

- In the busy highway of life, conflicts represent side alleys that are conspicuous, and at times, tempting. It is important to recognize that some of these alleys are dead ends, and an expedient retreat is critical. Some alleys represent a gateway to a greater cause and are worth pursuing, but never forget that the destination is the other highway and not the alley of conflict itself.

CONFLICT RESOLUTION
- The biggest requirement for long-lasting relationships is the mutual art of conflict resolution.

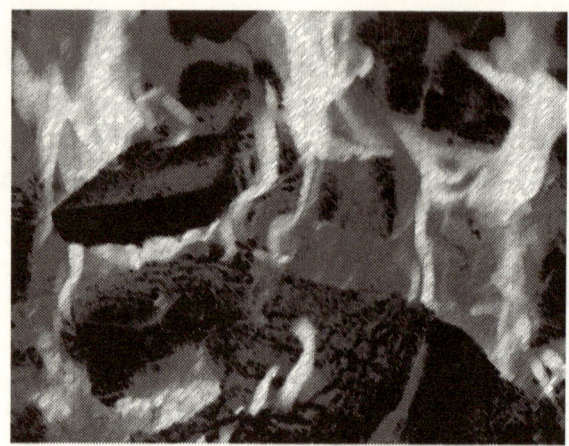

- Confinement is the first step to conflict resolution. What you cannot confine, you cannot resolve!
- Successful leaders know that, to resolve conflicts in the team, they must ensure that the cost of continued conflict exceeds the price of resolution for each of the team member.
- The biggest challenge to long-distance relationships is conflict resolution. There is something about face to face contact that demands resolution.
- Failing in timely confinement is to give life to a conflict. Place each conflict in a coffin of isolation and let time and isolation forge a resolution.

CONTEMPT

- Contempt is the predator that lurks within us, waiting to pounce on us at our weakest moment.

CONTENTMENT AND DISCONTENTMENT

- Before utopia can exist in this earth, it must exist in our minds. The human mind is incapable of harboring everlasting contentment.
- Hope is contagious.
- Habitual discontentment is demoralizing and may be contagious in any group. Successful managers differentiate it from situational discontentment and contain it effectively.
- Accept these three rules for a more contented life: Not everything needs be at your terms, as long as it is at acceptable terms. Not every gesture needs to be repaid, as long as it is recognized. Not every mistake needs to be punished, as long as it is rectified.
- Contentment will be achieved invariably if you focus on your share of choice and praise.
- Frustration cannot cease until you recognize that sometimes things do not work out and it is nobody's fault.
- The slogan of failure is "more time, more time"; and the slogan of success is "more opportunity, more opportunity." Discontentment does not differ between success and failure, only its roots.

CONTRIBUTION

- The contribution of any individual to society at large cannot be quantified without adjusting for confounders and interactions, using a multivariate analysis. However, the quality can be judged, because these adjustments in a model may change the magnitude, but rarely the positive or negative direction of the contribution.

CORRUPTION

- Corruption spreads through indirect contact transmission, where a susceptible person is infected from contact with a contaminated surface. To reduce transmission by indirect contact, frequent contact places should be properly disinfected.

CRACKS

- Cracks become irreversible crevices under pressure.

CRISIS MANAGEMENT

- Each crisis raises three sequential questions: what, why, and how? The sooner you get to the last question, the sooner you can develop a tangible solution.

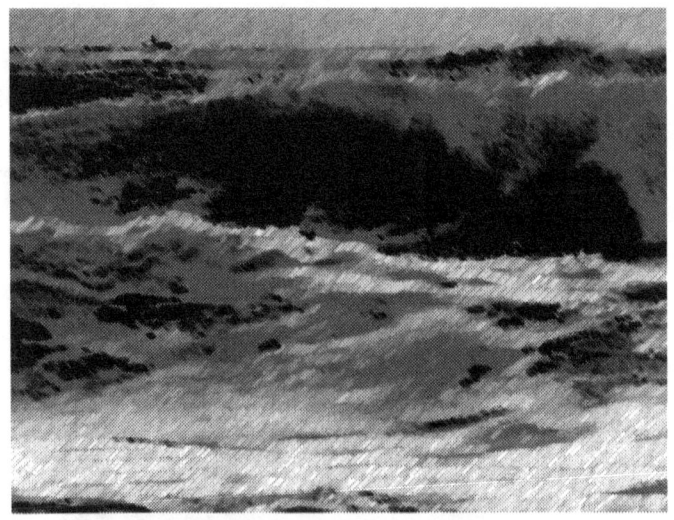

- The more intense the crisis, the sooner will it be over. You simply have to ride out a crisis as you would with a storm, while preserving vital resources.

CRITIQUE

- Critique is the chisel that shapes the statue of progress.
- It is not the strength of critique, but the sensitivity of the ears that determines its eventual impact.
- Do not underestimate the value of success, no matter how small, in interrupting mounting criticism.

CURIOSITY

- Necessity is the mother of invention, and curiosity is the mother of wisdom. Both are fathered by ambition.

- It is not curiosity but insecurity that killed the cat.

DEAL

- A deal is about granting unseen concessions in an assertive manner.

- The three most powerful words ever spoken are "deal with it."

DESIRE

- Beauty is in the eye, but desire is in the heart of the beholder.

DESTINY

- No one can control events. However, one can contain the loss and maximize the gain associated with each event, thus altering one's destiny.
- The term "hang in there" reflects our ill-founded belief that things will get better by themselves. In fact, our adaptation, rather than actual change of circumstances, accounts for most perceived improvement.
- Life is an open-labeled randomized trial, where each group has an equal chance of being randomized to adversity or favor. The process of randomization continues several times in everybody's lifetime.

DESPERATION
- In desperate times, cling hard and carefully to your end of the rope, or else it will end up being the noose around your neck.

DIPLOMACY
- Diplomacy is a room with many entrances and exits. It is a sanctuary that must not be desecrated by pride or prejudice.
- Vulnerability acts as a catalyst for diplomacy.

DISTORTION
- Distortion is the premier weapon of instigators.

DIVERSITY

- Diversity is the essence of life. We all prefer the colorful rainbow over the black-and-white one.
- Diversification is the death of monopolization, yet the birth of global dominance.

DREAMS
- Dreams cannot come true unless you are willing to accept them with the stains of reality.

EATING
- Eating remains underappreciated as a recreational activity, as talking remains underappreciated as a vocational activity.

- Recognize the value of effort independent of outcome. Every effort will become worthwhile, and happiness will come without effort.

- The enduring legacy of any effort or journey is not what we have achieved, but what we have become as a consequence. Therefore, the shortest efforts or journeys may not provide the most enduring legacies.
- Effort without vision is a waste, while vision without effort is futile.

- It is preferable to judge an action as "in the right or wrong direction" rather than declaring it "right or wrong." Declaring it as the latter ignores the dynamicity and flexibility in any action.
- Several endeavors in life are like fishing expeditions. However, it is important to know where to fish.
- Performance, not a title, is the best way to acquire and retain power.

- Progress may have been conceived when someone had an idea. However, progress was not born until someone decided to act on the idea.
- Effort without heart is like a honeymoon without a wife. It's neither a fun nor productive.
- In the marathon of life, our will is more likely to run out before our resources.

EMOTIONS
- Emotion can bring out the best and the worst in us. Intelligence will eventually be replicated by machines, but emotions will never be.
- Emotion is good slave, but a bad master in professional life, and vice versa in personal life.
- Emotional fatigue is as common as intellectual and physical fatigue, but frequently overlooked.

EXCESS

- Light obscures light, and dark obscures dark; excess is the enemy of prominence.

EXCELLENCE

- Excellence radiates like the sun. It will shine through thick and thin, and cannot be overshadowed by clouds of adversity.

EXCUSES

- Endless excuses by a victim of circumstances produce endless stories.

EXPANSION OF ORGANIZATION

- Each organization has a critical-mass threshold above which productivity loses cost- effectiveness. No expansion should be permitted prior to determining the critical-mass threshold.

EXPERIENCE

- Textbooks teach you to attend to what matters, and experience teaches you to ignore what does not matter.
- Experience is about learning from the consequences of your own decisions. It is not measured in years, but in the number and complexity of decisions.

EXTERNAL THREATS

- External threats are natural antidotes to internal disputes. If an external threat cannot unite a system, the system is beyond salvage.
- Outperforming the competition still remains the gold standard for winning in any sphere of life. Exploiting inner weaknesses and creating external threats for the competition has more theoretical appeal rather than practical value.

EXTREMISM
- Extremism is the mutant byproduct of "self-preservation" subsequent to failure or refusal to see things logically.

EVOLUTION
- Evolution is the bus that stops at every station and waits for everybody to get onboard. Its success is not in the pace, but in the all-embracing approach.

FACE
- A message without a face is like a child without a father. Messages born to anonymity lack appeal.

FALL
- Do not topple anything sitting on the wall, unless you are sure which side of the wall the object will fall on. Breaking the equilibrium is inducing instability and the results of instability are always unpredictable.

FAME

- Fame is similar to a galloping horse that can easily run out of control, and regardless, will tire down very quickly. Be sure to ride it on your terms and use it to ascend to a greater destination, quickly and effectively.
- The heat in the limelight constantly forces people to seek comfort in the shades of oblivion.

FAMILIARITY

- Familiarity is the road to acceptance.

FAVOR

- A favor is like a loan with unpredictable interest, payable on demand.

FATIGUE

- Fatigue is nature's way of ensuring that high-performing individuals leave the podium to give everyone else a chance.

FIGHT

- The fight of fights is the fight for the right to exist.

- Hide the skeletons of your fallen comrades, or else they will form stepping stones for your adversaries.

FIRST RESPONSE

- The first response may be an accurate one, but not

necessarily the most effective.

FITTING IN

- Our desire to "fit in" with any group or society may lead to an unnecessary demise of "self-identity." It is important to recognize that your contributions to the group or society are far more important of a determinant of "fitting in" than blind adaptation of existing behavioral patterns.

FLAG

- A flag symbolizes our undying faith that we stand for

something greater than ourselves.

FLEXIBILITY

- Flexibility is essential for dynamism. Water loses its dynamism when it freezes.
- Our flexibility in attitudes and joints reduces as we age, but we get better at avoiding situations demanding flexibility.

FREEDOM

- Freedom with accountability is the only freedom that should be allowed. This holds true for press, public, and children alike.

FRIEND

- A sincere friend would not let you make excuses for suboptimal performances. Success demands that you

have them readily available in your inner circle.
FUNERAL

- Each funeral leaves us with a sense of vulnerability to the inevitable and fears of missing the last ride to redemption.

FUTURE

- Sometimes you have to ignore the past and sacrifice the present to secure the future.

- The effect of any action is reflected on two axes: a place axis consisting sequentially of individual, group, and community; and time axis consisting sequentially of present, future, and even past.

GENEROSITY
- The generosity of a few can touch the lives of many. Never underestimate the wholesome effect of any generous action.

GLITTER

- Glitter has high sensitivity and low specificity, and thus it serves to identify but not select gold.

GREED
- Greed is ambition beyond moral limits.

GREATNESS
- Great systems are based on inflexible values and flexible strategies.

GOALS
- Choose high goals, but choose carefully. It is best to ignore what history will not remember.

GUARANTEE
- There are no guarantees in life; in fact, life itself is not guaranteed.

GUILT

- Guilt is the foul-but-fast stain that even escape from punishment cannot vanquish.

GYMNASIUM
- The gymnasium allows people to enjoy the addictive joy of achieving prime physical performance in controlled conditions.

HAND

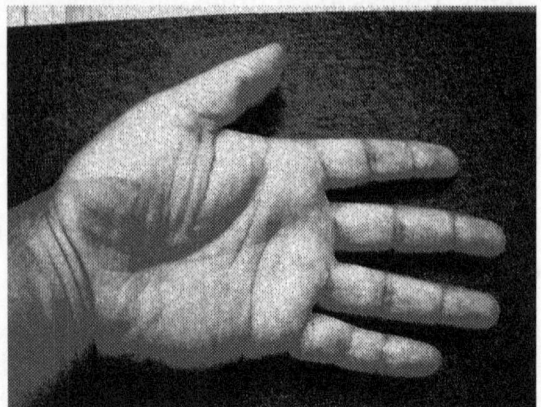

- A hand tells age better than a face because, it is spared by joys, worries, and makeovers.

HATRED

- Great fires of hatred can only be extinguished by internal resolve, not by external intervention.

HONOR

- It is better to lose with honor than to win without honor. Victories are leaves on a tree that last for a season, but honor is the trunk that defines the strength of a tree and ensures sustained strength for the times to come.

- A wounded body will heal by itself; a wounded pride only by vindication.

HOPE

- Hope is contagious. Man is both the host and vector for transmission of hope.
- Hope, belief, or obligation keeps us going every day. Frequently, we continue by sheer momentum, and sadly, lose sight of our aspirations.

HUMAN PSYCHE

- Within each of us lies a judge, a preacher, a student, and a victim. The relative contribution of each decides what we stand for.

HUMAN RIGHTS

- Human rights are not merely about existence, but about meaningful existence.

IGNORANCE

- Ignorance is not a consequence of the unseen, but of the unrecognized.

IMPORTANCE OF NEGATIVE PHENOMENA

- What would be the value of success without the existence of failure?
  What would be the value of compassion without the existence of adversity?
  What would be the value of knowledge without the existence of ignorance?
  What would be the value of health without the existence of sickness?
  What would be the value of life without the existence of death?

We keep forgetting that the things we detest most are the ones that provide value to our existence.

IN AND OUT

- Everything that goes in must come out, but not in the same configuration.

INCOMPETENCE

- Incompetence is like mud that sticks to your feet and shows throughout your path.
- The slogans of victimization have covered more products of incompetence than actual victims themselves.

INDECISIVENESS

- Indecisiveness is driven by uncertainty about decisions and reactions of other involved parties. Self-reliance is a powerful friend of decisiveness.

- Indecisiveness by us is a welcome to decisiveness by others. It remains a time-proven, guaranteed way to lose control.
- "Putting on hold" in most circumstances is a way to facilitate change in direction. In the other situations, it is a combination of indecisiveness, fear, and lack of confidence. Regardless, it remains one of the most frustrating states for those involved. Change the pace, but do not put on hold if you have any interest in moving any agenda forward.

INERTIA

- Mental inertia is the invisible roadblock to a beginning and an end.

INEVITABLY BAD

- Half-hearted effort, non-committal relationships, and insincere promises are all self-fulfilling prophecies. The negative effect of each on resource-utilization and morale cannot be underestimated.

INNER PEACE

- Inner peace is a divine gift given to those who prefer to give rather than take. It begs neither solitude nor comfort. It is the greatest gift of all, sought by many, but granted to only a deserving few.

INSECURITY

- Insecurity is distorted sense of vulnerability that hides behind the guise of excuse and blame.

INTERPRETATION

- What does the sign "=" indicate?

Two lines moving in the same direction!

Two lines moving in opposite direction!

Two lines that can never come together!

Two lines that look similar to each other!

One line is superior to the other!

How different are the interpretations for the same fact!

- To judge in haste is to judge unfairly. Just because somebody does not smile at you does not mean that he hates you. More likely, he simply does not know you.

INSTINCT

- Instinct is the subconscious marriage between desire, fear, and logic.

INTEGRATION

- Lateral integration, although challenging, is a great ally to vertical integration in any organization.

JUDGE

- To judge fairly is to judge achievement outside the shadows of expectation.

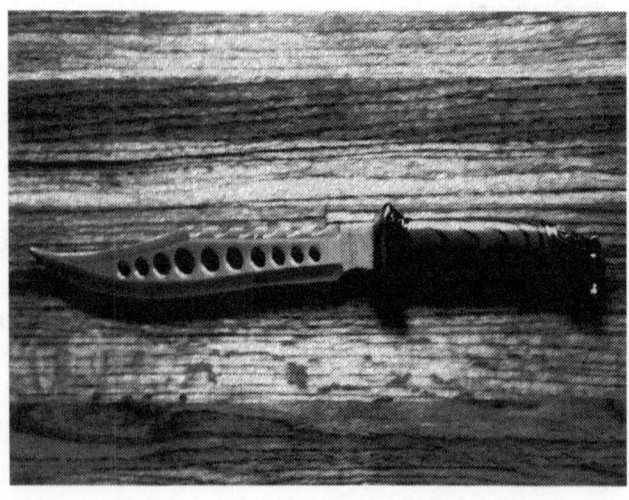

KEY

- The key is mightier than the pen or the sword. None has guarded the vaults of spiritual and material elements with the same valor and determination as the key itself. None has been sought with the same fervor by good and bad alike.

KNOWLEDGE

- The most valuable knowledge is not available in textbooks; it can be acquired only by active participation in the day-to-day life. Reading alerts one to what can only be learned by participation and interaction.

LEADERSHIP

- Self-doubt is a value great leaders cherish. It is an essential defense against the self-destructive "god complex."
- Great leadership starts with the statement "I accept responsibility." Self-empowerment starts with the sentence "I chose my destiny"; success starts with the sentence "I dare to lose."
- Great leadership requires mastering the art of confessing to mistakes without getting off the podium of strength. No mistakes should be confessed without a message of

unwavering determination and great hopes.

- Successful leaders must be secure enough to let others grow around them so that their legacy may continue. Nurture smaller trees instead of overshadowing them.

- A great leader serves as a beacon of light that attracts attention in a manner that highlights the contributions of each of the constituents of the team.
- The "rags-to-riches" story has more public appeal than the "greater-than-life" leaders. People only derive inspiration if they can see themselves playing the main character in any drama of life.
- Successful graduation to leadership requires the

completion of five core curriculum items:
-Confronting external challenges
-Resolving internal disputes
-Admitting to mistakes
-Sharing credit
-Implementing changes

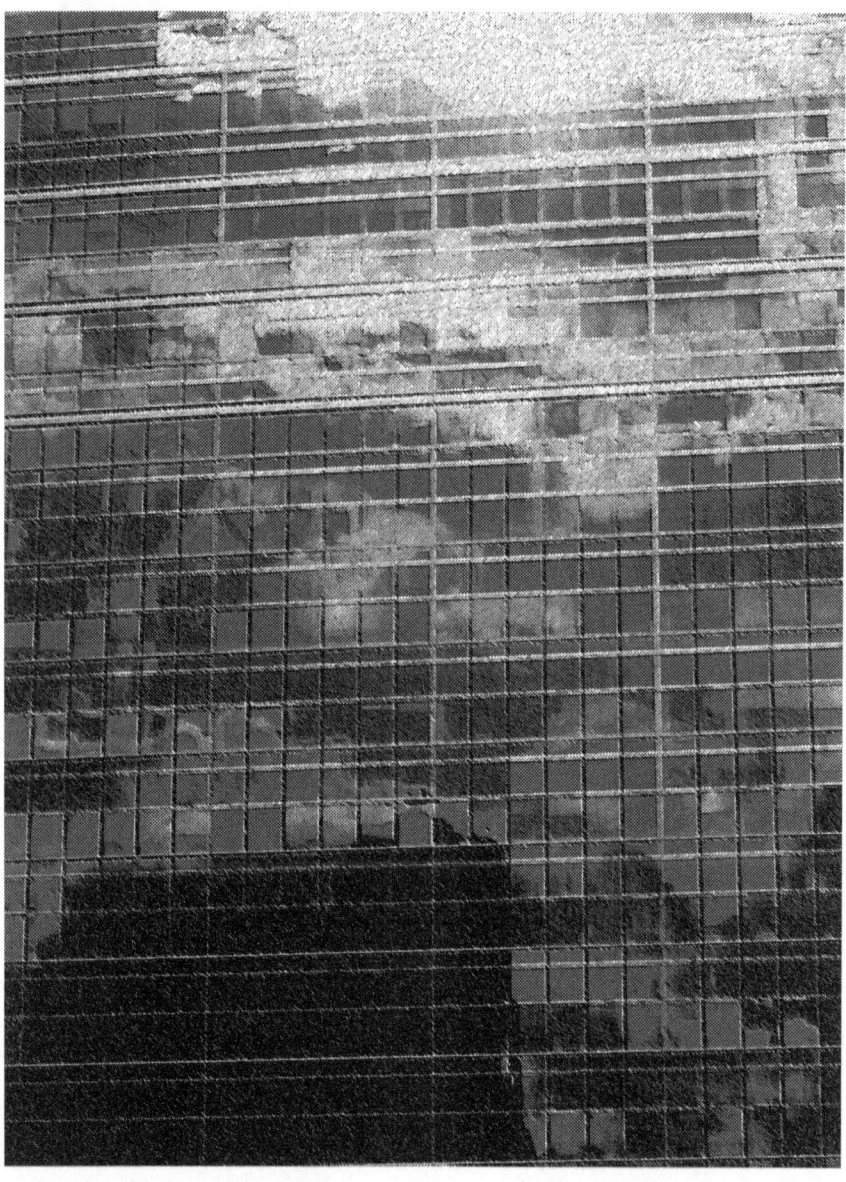

- Our leaders are a far greater a reflection of us than we recognize. It is wrong to blame the leadership without blaming ourselves.

- Each step forward is challenged by an unstable balance between immediate fears and distant hopes. A leader's conviction is essential to stabilizing this balance.

- Only a true leader can stand the test of time and tide against all odds for an unseen virtue.
- A leader can "bring it together" and "hold it together," but he or she must have something to "gather."
- A great person is judged by his success; a great leader by the success of his followers.

- All efficient managers are efficient workers first.
- Forgive the sincere mistakes of your followers like your mentors did yours.
- Only the greatest leader can walk away from power for the love of his people.
- Leadership should be driven by purpose, not by desire; conversely, love should be driven by desire, and not by purpose.
- The message of a great statesman continues to echo in our hearts and minds long after it is heard.

- A great leader does not commit for the people, he commits with the people. A great leader sees himself as an extension of his people, and then as something more.
- Great leaders carry an aura of invincibility; not about themselves, but about the cause they fight for.

- A great leader looks at his followers not as what they are but what they can be.

- True leadership has many styles, but only one purpose: to commit to the impossible and rest no more until the mission is completed. It begs no recognition nor price, but only and above all the inner pride that can only be achieved by delivering the promised.

LOSS

- Every competitive loss requires a non-competitive oath;
  I believe in the fairness of the outcome, regardless of the
  results; I wholeheartedly accept my loss, only as one of
  many events to come, and nothing more; I will not accept
  that someone is willing to work harder and sacrifice more
  than I can, and I will not rest until redemption is mine.
  If I cannot commit to this oath, it is time to quit and seek
  peace in oblivion.
- Every situation is salvageable, provided you do not
  care about the harshness of the choices; the worse the
  situation, the harder the choices.

LOVE
- Our fascination with pets and children is a reflection of our need for unconditional love.
- True love and respect are both blind to prejudice, but not to each other.

LOYALTY AND INTEGRITY
- Endless loyalty does not exist, but endless integrity does. Choose integrity over loyalty, and you will find an enduring relationship.

MARRIAGE
- Marriage is the purest form of an unconditional merger that remains poorly understood, yet widely respected and sought.

MODERN MEDICINE

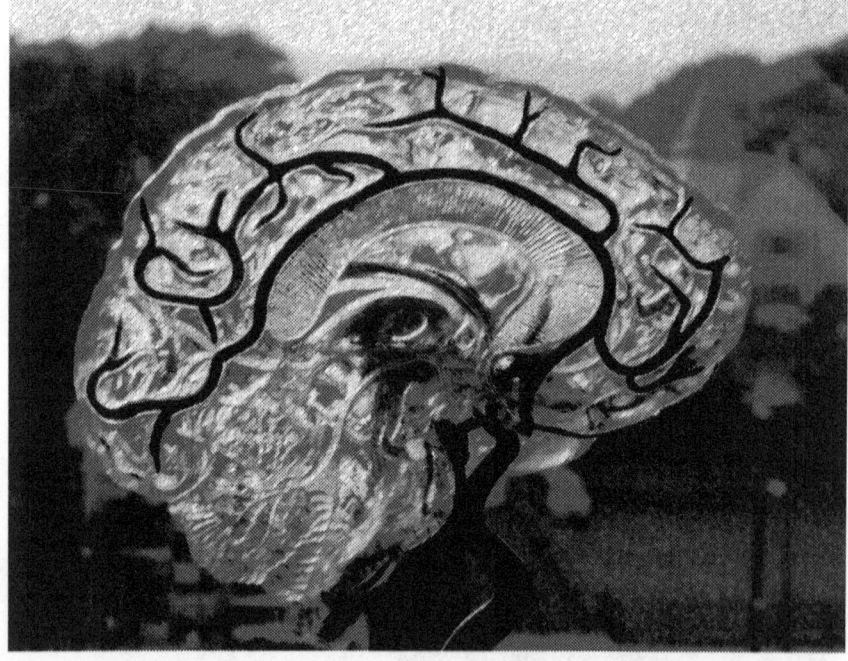

- Modern medicine, by saving lives, has brought mankind to face the greater threat of disability. Modern medicine must ask itself whether there is more to medicine than saving lives.
- In medicine, as in life, you must be prepared to help many to save a few.

MORTALITY

- Mortality may be the greatest gift to man yet. Imagine the enthusiasm for an endless journey.

NEGOTIATION

- Successful negotiators must possess the ability to convince the other party that items of perceived unilateral interest are actually items of bilateral interest, and that the perceived value of items is higher than the actual value.
- Successful negotiations require identification of four elements *a priori*:
  -The negotiable component
  -The non-negotiable component
  -Points of synergy
  -Points of controversy

- Act as a door, not as a wall, for new ideas. Maintain the sensitive equilibrium between time and space. Not every new idea can be accommodated in the same place at the same time.
- Each idea initially circulates in a closely knit circle. Successful ideas do not leave the circle; the circle just gets bigger.

- Remember, opportunities linger around you, even in moments of despair and hardship. Winners are not those who "get" good opportunities, but are those who "avail" them.

ORGANIZATION

- Any organization that commits to self-sacrifice for the greater good has already taken the first step to greatness. This commitment will bind them together into an eternal legacy that will last longer than their mortal existence.
- The same characteristics that build and maintain an empire may not be enough to save it in a time of crisis.

- In theory, new faces are not required to generate and implement new thoughts. Although new faces have become the symbol of new thoughts, their biggest contribution is the new will that they bring with them to any organization.
- A merger brought by necessity, unlike that brought by ideology, is short-lived.

OUTCOME

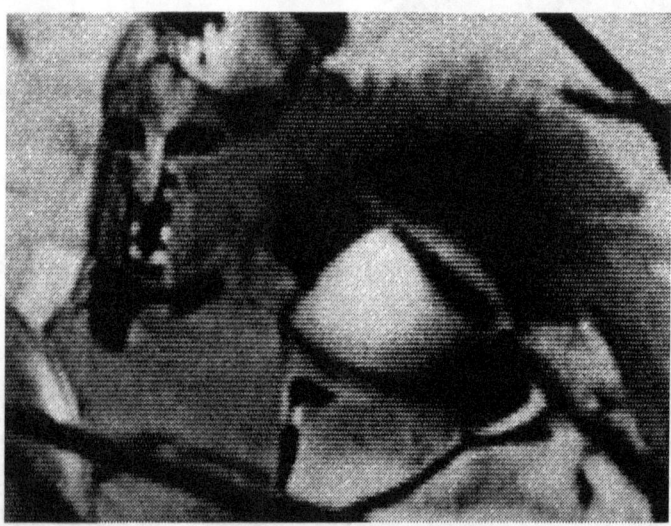

- All acts can be justified, but consequences, not justification, will eventually determine the place of any action on the mantle of history.

PERSEVERANCE

- Learn from your disappointments and develop perseverance. Disappointments turn into failures only if you refuse to learn or persist.

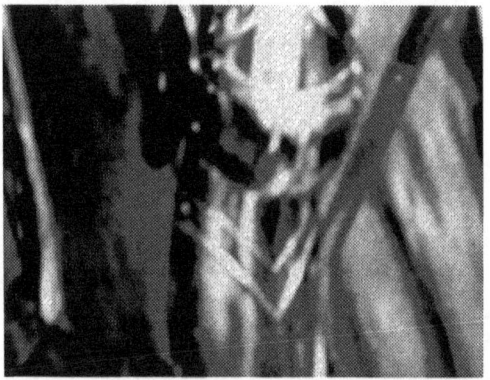

- Brilliance attracts, but persistence recruits.

POLITICS

- Politics is the art of achieving goals with minimum conflict or confrontation. Great leaders and great politicians alike have used it. However, great leaders have used this art for achieving selfless goals.

POWER

- Power is, in reality, control over freedom, finances, and fraternity. It is not how much power you have, but how much power you can exert not only on others but on yourself.

PRACTICAL

- Practical is the middle point between "easy to do" and ideal.

- The picture of reality is made by the paintbrush of practicality on the canvas of theory. Theory and practice are inseparably superimposed in the realm of reality.

PRESS

- Press is the conduit of knowledge, with many crossroads. A good journalist holds knowledge divine above desecration from personal prejudices. A great journalist convinces the readers to hold knowledge divine above desecration by personal prejudices.

PREVENTION

- Prevention is the curtain that hides its own show. The more effective the prevention, the less spectacular the dance of feared events on the stage of life.

PRIDE

- Pride can only be seen as a reflection, either through a

mirror, or through the faces of people closest to us.

- Instant gratification runs like an epidemic in the third world. It is borne by uncertainty and can only be eradicated by instilling pride in one's existence.

PRODUCTIVITY

- While one may be born with superior intelligence, the relationship between intelligence and productivity is not linear. At highest levels of intelligence, productivity suffers, due to lack of focus and the perceived union between practice and theory. Therefore, the most intelligent people are not necessarily the most successful people in this realm.
- All efficient workers are hard workers, but all hard workers may not be efficient.

PROFESSIONAL COMPETITION

- In the arduous professional journey, it is inevitable that some of your closest colleagues will turn against you. This change in direction will be brought about by differences in ideology, circumstances, and new needs. Accept it as part of the journey and part with them early, on favorable terms. Parting early is hard, but parting late is destructive.
- As you move up the ladder, competition increases not in quantity, but in quality.

PROPER PERSPECTIVE

- Most situations in life are polygonal, not spherical. Depending upon your point of view, a different image is visualized. Consider multiple points of view to get a comprehensive understanding of the situation.
- The only way to address any issue appropriately is to focus on it. However, beware that no issue stands alone, and it is a mistake to consider any issue in isolation.

RANDOMIZATION

- Randomization is the process of unpredictable allocation driven by chance.

REASSURANCE

- Reassuring others is the best form of self-assurance. Respecting others is the best form of self-respect. Healing others is the best form of self-healing. Motivating others is the best form of self-motivation. Selflessness, at times, is the key to self-serving goals.

RELATIONSHIP

- The difference between "partnership" and "relationship" is the magnitude and quality of expected reciprocity. Sacrifice without expectation of reciprocation is the hallmark of "relationships."

RESPECT VERSUS POPULARITY

- Choose respect over popularity. Popularity waxes and wanes. Only respect lasts beyond a lifetime.

RESPONSE

- No response is a response with many faces; no to a request and yes to a questionable action.
- You do not have to be right all the time. To be successful, being right half of the time is adequate. For a quarter, people are willing to forgive. For the remaining quarter, no one else knows the right answer, either.

- When people are testing the water around your island, do not leave your response to chance.
- Seeking the right answer without asking the right question is like fishing without a hook and bait.

REVOLUTION
- Revolution is rebellion with a soul of purpose.

ROCK BOTTOM

- The term hitting the rock bottom is a misnomer because it overlooks the several invisible layers of disappointments that exist beneath what is visible.

RHYTHM

- Rhythm is the pulse of music, and pulse is the rhythm of life.

SACRIFICE

- Every notable sacrifice in history was, in fact, an investment for a better future.
- You do not become an integral part of a group until you sacrifice personal gain for the betterment of the group.

SEARCH FOR GOD

- The search for God is actually a search for virtues existing within us.

SEARCH FOR HEROES

- Every time you ask the question "where are the heroes?"; look in the mirror and not outside the window.

SELF-INTEREST

- What you put on nature's plate must be a healthy mixture of self-serving and selfless products. Neither is sustainable alone.

SELF-RELIANCE

- If I were to choose from fame, fortune, opportunity, luck, or self-reliance, I would choose self-reliance. That is the only thing that endures.
- Reliance on others must die before the self-reliance within us can live.

SELFISHNESS VERSUS KINDNESS

- Kind is the one who does something for people that they would not do for him; considerate is the one who does something for people that they would do for him; selfish is the one who would not do something for people that they would do for him.

SERMONS

- Any sermon that highlights the differences between and within religions and not similarities is not a sermon, but exploitation.

SHADOW OF DOUBT

- Excessive doubt can hinder successful pursuits in life. Inevitably, every time light is shed on an object, a dark shadow appears. Never forget that the active ingredient in the image is the object, and not the shadow.

SHIFTING OF ANGER

- The transfer of anger and fault to the individuals closest to us is common, but not a benign defensive reflex. Share the pain without the element of anger and guilt.

SHRINE

- A shrine is a testament, not to the past, but to the future. If someone did it before, someone will do it again.

SINCERITY

- Sincerity is the sense of duty that exists without the concomitant existence of reward or punishment.

SINS

- Whenever we pay for our sins, it is on someone else's terms.

SMALL STEPS

- Advancement in life comprises numerous small steps and occasional giant leaps. Never underestimate the importance of small steps; they constitute the overwhelming bulk of overall advancement, and they also provide the momentum for giant leaps.

SMILE

- A smile is a gesture of friendship that will never be obsolete.

SORROW

- Tears of sorrow must never put out the fire of inspiration that burns within us. In fact, the fire must dry the tears.

STABILITY
- Stability begets stability. You cannot pull people out of troubled water while you are balancing on a tightrope.

STABLE MARRIAGE
- Acceptance of differences is the hallmark of stable marriages; after all, a wife can offer a greater alignment of interests than friends can.

STATISTICS
- Statistics are the numerical expression of the obvious.

STATUS QUO

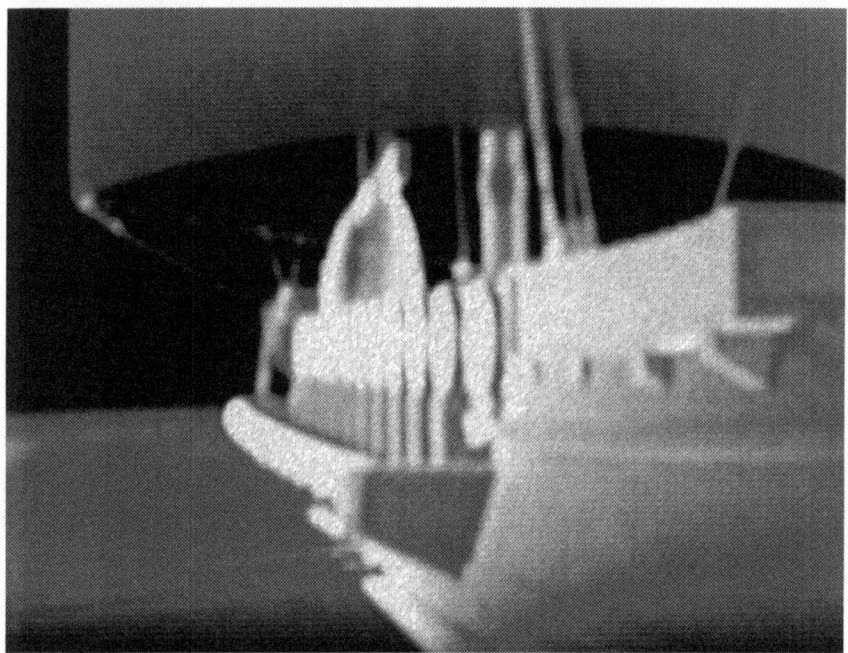

- Status quo is the ship that is in the harbor but is unable to dock or voyage out. It is unproductive as an entity, and it is also obtrusive to other ships.

STRESS
- Stress is a non-linear, internal response to external pressure.

SUCCESS AND FAILURE
- In a world that is dynamic, success is highly dependent upon knowing the right time and place for tomorrow, not just for today.

- There is no fixed formula for success, and there will never be one. The basic ingredients of desire, effort, and persistence must be mixed in variable proportions subservient to the demands of time and place. The purpose of meeting successful people is to derive inspiration and not to seek the method for success.
- The most common reason for failure is undertaking too many tasks at one time. Never expand the number of tasks prior to expanding the infrastructure.

- The legacy of any spectacular ascent in any sphere of life cannot be immortalized without a timely and graceful descent.
- Previous success supports, but does not guarantee future success.
- Accepting defeat is hard, living with it harder.
- Failure is a stepping stone for success, provided you learn a lesson from it.
- At times, not losing is as good as winning.

- Fragments of yesterday's shattered dreams may be the raw material for tomorrow's conquests.
- Stepping down at the right time is the only way to escape being brought down at the wrong time.

- Any gain acquired without effort is not worthy of possession. It is like a flower without the mother plant; it will whither away quickly on its own and you will not be able to acquire another one.
- There is no "I" in "success," but a "u" and "s." There is an "I" in "failure," but it contains four other letters: "L," "I," "F," and "E." Failure requires not just recognition of individual responsibility, but its coexistence with life.
- Controversy and success are inseparable in their existence, but may lag behind each other in an unpredictable sequence.
- The pendulum of life oscillates between success and failure. The greater the swing of the pendulum towards success, the greater the inevitable mirror oscillation in the other direction.

- Life oscillates between high and low points. Oscillations can masquerade or obscure trends in favorable and unfavorable directions. Most oscillations, unlike trends, do not need a change in strategy. Identify and follow the midpoint of oscillations to avoid overzealous response or failure to respond.
- Success is the carrot in front of the donkey. It is a self-perpetuating cycle: new carrot, same donkey; or same carrot, new donkey.

SPECTATOR SPORT

- For successful people, life is not a spectator sport. However, the drama of life is increasingly becoming a spectator sport. The media, over the centuries, has not increased the number of players per capita, but augmented the number of spectators per capita, several-fold. The proportion of news that is read or heard throughout the world, without any personal relevance, is a living testament to this issue.

SUNRISE AND SUNSET

- Sunrise is inspiring, as it signifies a new beginning; and sunset is comforting, as it offers the chance of a new beginning.

TACTICIAN

- A master tactician always retains the initiative, even in moments of despair, by treating every adversity as an opportunity.

TAKEN FOR GRANTED

- "Taken for granted" is a relationship in which the down-payment is done, but ownership is assumed prior to completing the installments.

TALENT

- True talent cannot remain in the confines of obscurity forever. It will eventually find its way to center stage, even if a stage has to be built around it.

TEACHERS

- All great teachers were great students. In fact, great teachers never stop being great students.
- Teaching or healing others is a sublime activity.

- A mentor not only projects his or her student's talents to the world, but augments them, several-fold.

- Reward, punishment, and example remain the foundations of teaching. Experienced teachers and parents know the value of individualized, balanced proportions with periodic updates.

TEAM

- A good team is like a household. Every member often works outside the framework of his direct responsibility. A great team does not discern between responsibilities among each other; they accept it as their overall responsibility.

- Each team member represents a piece of a jigsaw puzzle. Each piece, irrespective of its size, is equally essential for completion of the puzzle.

TEMPTATION
- Temptation is opportunity sought without need, then pursued without ethics.

TIME

- Time is the worst executioner and the best humanitarian of them all. It will spare none in its path, and it is unstoppable; yet it may be the best salvation for many of us.

TRUST
- Trust everybody, and life will be impractical; but trust nobody and life will be unbearable.

- Acquaintance must precede affection, and sincerity must precede trust.

TRUTH
- Truth always survives centuries of challenges, and it eventually prevails.
- Digging for the truth is more likely to weed out the perceived truth than uncover new truth.

UNCERTAINTY
- Uncertainty has a remarkable ability for metamorphoses and metastases everywhere.

UNIVERSE

- We recognize half of what exists around us; we understand about a quarter; and we utilize only a fraction of what exists around us.

UNTHINKABLE
- Unthinkable by one is not inconceivable by another.

VALUABLE
- The most valuable items in life are bought before they are auctioned.

VISION AND DEDICATION

- Vision and dedication are complements, and not substitutes for each other.

VISIONARY

- A visionary is someone who would invest in a venture with no expected returns during his or her lifetime.

<u>VICTORY</u>
- Any expensive victory that does not bring you any closer to your ultimate goal will eventually feel like a defeat.

<u>VULNERABILITY</u>
- He who preys on the vulnerability of others has chosen Satan's daughter for a bride.

<u>WAR AND PEACE</u>

- The ravages of war are the greatest cry for peace.

- Unfortunately, the cost of war, rather than the morality of cause, has defined the resolve to go to war.

WISDOM

- Wisdom is the code book that enables us to decipher nature's messages, which exist all around us. This book, however, cannot be bought or sold; it has to be compiled, bit by bit, from visible sources, with pain-staking efforts.
- Wisdom is the altruistic interpretation of common knowledge.

WORLD ORDER

- The new world order is really a new name for the old world order. How many new ways can there be for a group of few to control the destiny of many?

- Subduing nations requires hiding from them not what they cannot do, but what they can do. Unfortunately, the most subduing comes from within, not outside.

WORD AND ACTION

- Do not proclaim what you cannot demonstrate.

Dr. Qureshi is Professor of Neurology, Neurosurgery, and Radiology and the Executive Director of the Stroke Center at University of Minnesota, Minneapolis. Three years ago, he founded the Zeenat Qureshi Stroke Research Center that continues to perform cutting edge research in developing new treatments for stroke. His book is a compilation of quotations, related to all spheres of life, generated from years of learning from mentors, circumstances, and eventually students. This book is not a message but a tool of inspiration to unravel messages that exist around us at all times. It is a reminder to all of us that ignorance is not a consequence of the unseen, but of the unrecognized. It is an attempt to pass from one hand to another, the most valued gift of all, the core of wisdom.

www.ingramcontent.com/pod-product-compliance
Lightning Source LLC
Chambersburg PA
CBHW031258280526
45784CB00004B/1893